# We Walk by Faith

## Michael Demkovich, OP

## NEW PRIORY PRESS

EXPLORING THE DOMINICAN VISION

**Lumen Library
Collection**

Scripture quotations are from *The Catholic Edition of the Revised Standard Version of the Bible*, copyright © 1965, 1966 National Council of the Churches of Christ in the United States of America. Used by permission. All rights reserved.

Quotations from the *Catechism of the Catholic Church* (English translation copyright © 1994, United States Catholic Conference, Inc. – Liberia Editrice Vaticana) are indicated with the abbreviation *CCC* followed by the paragraph citation.

*Imprimi potest*

Very Rev. James V. Marchionda, O.P.
Prior Provincial Province of St. Albert the Great, USA
Dominican Friars

Photo credits: The Konza Prairie Hiking Trail, Manhattan, Kansas, by Michael Demkovich, O.P.

# Dedication

For the cloistered nuns
throughout the world,
especially for
my Dominican sisters.

After too many centuries of a static understanding of the God-human relationship, Michael Demkovich offers us a profound journey language that mirrors—and deepens—the spiritual path that we actually walk. This is pastoral theology at its best!

**Fr. Richard Rohr,O.F.M.**
Center for Action and
Contemplation
Box 12464
Albuquerque, New Mexico 87195

The Christian life has been described as a journey to God. In fact, there are many shorter journeys within our lifetime that make up the story of our path to holiness. Michael Demkovich has offered us just such a mini-journey for seven days to accompany the pilgrim who is walking by faith. Listen to his stories as you ponder the spiritual narrative that is being revealed in you.

**Fr. Harry M. Byrne, O.P.**
Professor Emeritus – Pastoral
Theology & Spiritual Direction
Aquinas Institute of Theology
St. Louis, MO 63108

# Table of Contents

# WE WALK BY FAITH

# Foreword

One of my favorite verses from poetry is in T.S. Eliot's *Little Gidding*: "We shall not cease from exploration and the end of all our exploring will be to arrive where we started and know the place for the first time." Father Michael Demkovich's new book, *We Walk by Faith*, is fast becoming my favorite spiritual guide on my journey, my exploration, of faith. Tracing the journeys of our spiritual ancestors to such places as Egypt and Emmaus, Jerusalem and Jericho, to name a few, Father Demkovich marks out possible paths our own inner exploring may take as we follow the Lord Jesus on the most important journey of all, the journey of faith. Inviting us to walk more closely with the Lord, who is "the Way, the Truth and the Life," this gem of a book will open up for the reader the Word of God, who is Christ the Lord, and in whose heart all journeys begin and end. Father Demkovich invites us to return from each of these chapters, these pilgrim paths, pondering their meaning in our lives and coming to know our starting place as if "for the first time." All journeys require guidance of some sort, whether a traditional map or a high-tech GPS. This spiritual guide persuades us that the most reliable compass is faith, a faith nurtured by the One who travels with us always.

**Most Reverend John C. Wester**
Archbishop of Santa Fe
4000 St. Joseph Place, NW
Albuquerque, New Mexico 87120

WE WALK BY FAITH

# Introduction

Throughout history the themes of journey, quest, and pilgrimage have captured our imaginations especially in religious circles and for good reason. To journey, the simple act of walking, we simultaneously take leave of one place and encounter a new one, it is both a letting-go and an embracing. Anticipation and expectation for the new, for what might be, and a certain realization and appreciation for what is. It is no less true in the spiritual life and this little devotional work will demonstrate this.

When we think of the spiritual life as a journey we open ourselves to the dynamic reality of motion, that is to say life. We journey from the old self, to new possibilities, from the potential "may be" to the actual "it is." Now, not all journeys involve travel, or distances. More often the most significant journeys are the ones that are within, the *exitus* and *reditus* of life, the going out that returns more aware. It is a journey that comes full circle with new understanding. In this little book I encourage you to hear this journey with your inner ear. The true gift of the spiritual cloister is the enclosure of the inner self. In this enclosure, we must meet our true self. Catherine of Siena described it as "the cell of self-knowledge." For many people this journey of stillness is difficult, especially given the over-stimulation of social media.

In the pages that follow I invite you on a spiritual journey, to walk more closely with our Lord. The New Testament is full of stories about journey, being on the way (*in via*) with the Lord. We will take seven such walks, a week of spiritual journeys. I encourage you to read this book in daily doses, one chapter for each day. You may even wish to use this book with a group as a weekly source of reflection and meditation. Whatever works best for your journey is what I recommend.

Each day holds its own spiritual terrain and invites you to the interior life, wherein one finds the depth meaning of one's life. Our journeys are to Bethlehem, Egypt, Jericho, Jerusalem, Emmaus, Damascus and Gaza. They are journeys that bring us to the prophetic, the alien, the merciful, the salvific, the well-traveled, the repentant, and the desert roads of life. As you can see, they take us to the heart of the Christian life. Each journey is a walk with the Lord, a time to encounter the trails and traces of the heart. It is ideal if you end each chapter with some time to reflect, to meditate, for the chapters in this little book are best read as distinct passages, textual as well as spiritual adventures. As with any journey we engage it even before we leave. Each journey begins with a passage from the Bible. I invite you to take time to prayerfully and deeply hear God's word before embarking on each journey. [You may prefer to use your own Bible instead of the translation I have provided.] One spiritual writer advises that journeys unfold in three stages "preparation and anticipation, journey and return."[1] I encourage you to see each chapter as such travel. First anticipate it in reading the Scripture passage; engage the journey as you read each reflection; and return at the end of each chapter as you ponder its meaning in your life. It is important that you read the Scriptural passage so that each chapter's journey will be richer in meaning, and your own reflections more rewarding. Even though the Scripture may be familiar and the temptation is to fly through it, I advise against it. Take your time.

---

[1] Robin Daniels *The Virgin Eye, Toward a Contemplative View of Life* (Instant Apostle; 2016) p. 103.

## INTRODUCTION

I would like to express my thanks to the Dominican nuns at the Monastery of the Angels in Hollywood, California. They are an amazing group of women whose faith and cloistered life of prayer is an inspiration. This book grew out of a retreat I gave to them and I appreciate their inviting me to share my thoughts on the spiritual life. I am also thankful to the various people who read a draft of this work and offered comments and observations that greatly helped the final product: Donna Burns, Kimberlee Kavasch, Joan See, Fr. Harry Byrne, O.P., Msgr. J. Bennet Voorhies, Fr. Ron Wasikowski. Finally, I would like to thank the Dominican Province of St. Albert the Great for affording me time to be able to complete this project.

# WE WALK BY FAITH

# Chapter 1: Journey to Bethlehem: The Prophetic Road

*Mary was grave with child*

This journey to Bethlehem is the first and greatest mystery of God since it is into the depth of the Incarnation. The Evangelist Luke tells us of the first journey of trust and promise. It is the journey of Joseph and Mary at a time of census and a time of confinement, for Mary was pregnant with child. Read Luke 2:1–7.

### The Birth of Jesus

1 In those days a decree went out from Emperor Augustus that all the world should be registered. 2 This was the first registration and was taken while Quirinius was governor of Syria. 3 All went to their own towns to be registered. 4 Joseph also went from the town of Nazareth in Galilee to Judea, to the city of David called Bethlehem, because he was descended from the house and family of David. 5 He went to be registered with Mary, to whom he was engaged and who was expecting a child. 6 While they were there, the time came for her to deliver her child. 7 And she gave birth to her firstborn son and wrapped him in bands of cloth, and laid him in a manger, because there was no place for them in the inn. (*NRSVCE*)

As we see in this passage our first journey is into the mystery of the Incarnation. The Christmas story seems welcome if not out of place at any time but winter. However, it is the story of an amazing woman of faith who said "yes" to God's will. Her *fiat voluntas tua*, "thy will be done" is the receptive soul wherein the Word of God takes flesh. So too, in the spiritual life, we must open ourselves to receive the

Word. Out of our poverty, God acts *ex utero Virgini*, "from the womb of the Virgin" and this is echoed in our lives of Faith. In our lack, our chaste purity or spiritual virginity we are open to life itself. The sanctity of the womb is revealed in God's choice to be born like all mortal flesh. It is for this reason that the Church so consistently defends the dignity of the unborn and the sanctity of matrimony, for in both, the divine breaks into our world. Sadly our world has lost its way and it must be called back to Bethlehem as we sort out the confusion.

Truly the Incarnation is the birthing of the divine and the fourteenth century Dominican mystic Meister Eckhart rightly describes our Christian lives as being midwives in this birth.[2] But midwifery is a messy business. Not that I have first-hand knowledge, but I do know that spiritual midwifery is dramatic and immersed in the stuff of life. The birth of our Lord did not happen in the familiar and comfortable, but it came to be by civil and secular decree, Mary and Joseph were made displaced persons, leaving their home in Galilee, traveling to Judea and the town of Bethlehem, the city of David. This journey opens the way within where we may encounter God.

There is a certain spiritual dislocation, being uprooted from our homeland, our self-centeredness; the places of our past ancestry which also hold our future destiny. Our spiritual journey to Bethlehem is a letting go of what is untrue about our deepest self. It is an honest encounter with our past and our future. As pilgrims, our journey to Bethlehem means that we are called to our ancestral home, the charism of our life. One's personal history, one's ability

---

[2] *Meister Eckhart: The Essential Sermons, Commentaries, Treatises, and Defense*. Edmund Colledge & Bernard McGinn trans. (New York: Paulist Press; 1981) "Counsel on Discernment 4" p. 250.

to adapt to the realities of one's time, has kept the Catholic Faith fresh. The spiritual journey to Bethlehem reinvigorates our life. In this journey we walk with Joseph and Mary amid the world's uncertainty, trusting God's promise even if we have been summoned by imperial decree. We are made to leave our homes and journey to our past and we must register in our ancestral towns, to those spiritual places that our adult life has neglected or forsaken. We journey to the past to discover our future, our destiny. Like Joseph and Mary there is a new life entrusted to us and Mary teaches us an important lesson.

Our Lady invites us to discover the reality of being betrothed as well as being with child. You see, we must strive to share with others the fruit of the spiritual life. Mary unites us with her son for we are wedded to Christ. It is a unique gift of the Mother of God, to draw us more closely to her Son. I have seen countless individuals in the confessional weep as they encounter their wounded-ness and sense the nearness of Our Lady. I can honestly say my experience has been that Mary is ever so close to us when we are wounded, most vulnerable. We ought to seriously ponder Mary's role in healing the world's wounded-ness and ours. Her apparitions throughout history have met the wounds of humanity— Fatima, Lourdes, Guadalupe, Czestochowa—she calls us to her son. The journey to Bethlehem is about fulfillment, bringing us to the Nativity, but it is also about travail, challenge and struggle.

This journey to Bethlehem is cast in the historical moment of Caesar Augustus and the census of the world. Strange, that this journey is all about where we are from, our past, our places of origin. One would expect a great welcoming or homecoming but Mary and Joseph experienced mean and rough times, crowded and congested with no place of hospitality, of friendly welcome. The Roman census was to lay a burden on the people, the tax of Roman rule. Quirinius the governor of Syria is even named by Luke, so oppressive did this tax become. In one sense the burden of sin, symbolized in the occupation by Rome, marks all our journeys, for sin is the great tax imposed that weighs us down.

In our story from Luke notice that it is Mary, free from sin, who must journey amid a sinful nation to bring forth the Son of God, who will be Victor over Sin and Death. The journey to Bethlehem is one that is very healing, it is undertaken for the salvation of sinners. Only in a life that ponders the Word of God, that allows it to take flesh in us, do we have the courage to face the world with all its evil. The journey to Bethlehem must be a journey into the heart of contemplation.

I needed to give a talk to some first-year college students at their retreat and the theme was: "Be still and know that I am God." So many young people find contemplation, their being still, very difficult. It is for a very good reason that the Dominican Order's motto is *contemplare et contemplata aliis tradere* (to contemplate and to share with others the fruit of contemplation), for we know contemplation is ordered to the world, to our fellow sojourners, we contemplate in order to share the fruits of contemplation. All too often, especially in our Do! Do! Do! culture we dismiss the critical importance of being. Meister Eckhart wisely tells us: "We should not think that holiness is based on what we do but rather on who we are, for it is not our works which sanctify us but we who sanctify our works." The necessity of <u>doing life</u> very often eclipses the <u>being of life</u>. Many times I will ask a person in spiritual direction to take their hefty "to do" list and to compose alongside of it a "to be" list. Contemplation is about being, just plain old being. There is nothing more active than just simply being.

St. Thomas Aquinas, in his question on Christ's manner of life (*ST* III q.40) asked if Christ should have led a solitary life. Recall that for Thomas the most perfect life was the contemplative life so it would seem that solitude would be the life best suited to Christ. How often has anyone of us, during those moments of prayer when we are all alone, thought "Gee isn't this great." Then the door opens, the phone rings or someone comes calling, ruining the whole thing. As Sartre said, "Hell is other people" or from Charlie Brown, Linus' declaring, "I love humanity, it's people I can't stand." Both attitudes fail to appreciate that the journey to Bethlehem gives birth to the Savior of the World, an essentially humane mission.

Solitude, while perhaps conducive to contemplation, is not the manner of life for Christ, especially given his mission and purpose, namely: first, to bear witness to the truth; second, to free us from sin and third, to offer to us access to God. Thomas' reply to the second objection states: "Absolutely speaking the contemplative life is more perfect than the active, because the latter is taken up with bodily actions." But Thomas makes a distinction that is so important when it comes to contemplation. He says "...yet that form of active life in which a person by preaching and teaching, delivers to others the fruits of contemplation, is more perfect than the life that stops at contemplation for it is built on an abundance of contemplation." Our contemplation is fruitful, it is very pregnant! Our entire mission must be born of this fruitful contemplation.

The journey to Bethlehem is our call to be contemplatives for the world, to share with others because of an abundance that must be shared. Mary is our model of contemplation, one who is pregnant with the Word of God. It isn't enough for us just to dabble in contemplation, no we must bear fruit. While Christ is the perfection of this contemplation, we follow him and though perhaps not perfectly, we do strive to build our lives on the abundance of contemplation. My niece was in her second trimester and I saw a picture, she was very pregnant. As contemplatives we are pregnant with God's word, and we should be large with life. In vocal and mental prayer, meditation and contemplative prayer, these are all ways that prayer takes flesh (*CCC* 2700)[3]. St. Therese talks of contemplation as "a close sharing of friends" and St. Ignatius of Loyola spoke of it as a fixed gaze of faith—"I look at him and he looks at me." St. John of the Cross calls it "silent prayer" (2709, 2715, and 2717). How easy it is for us not to contemplate, to not behold the face of the beloved. The root meaning of the word "contemplation," is "to mark out the space for us to gaze attentively." The journey to Bethlehem reaches its two-fold goal: the birth of God or the Nativity, and secondly our adoration, our intensely seeing the mystery of God. However, like the Magi and the Holy Family we may not dwell but must journey yet again.

## Take Time to Ponder

Here we come to the end of this journey and the importance of taking some time to ponder this day's journey. For some the interior life is easily undertaken due to age and the lessons of life that dispose a person to genuine self-awareness. Often times growing old can school a person in sensing the outer life and inner life. Illness or convalescence too can impress upon a person, whether they are young or

---

[3] *Catechism of the Catholic Church* (Ligouri Publications, 1993).

old, a profound sense of genuineness and personal integrity. While this is true, many of us can find it challenging to enter into the stillness of the human heart. Busy work schedules, kids' sporting events, social engagements, club or committee meetings, cable television, video games and social media all create distraction and static that makes it hard to enter the stillness. If you find the stillness difficult, then this section on pondering may be a bit challenging. I suggest that you take time to find a quiet place, focus on your heart beat or your breathing and allow yourself to slowly sink within where you are aware of genuineness and authenticity. This is a contemplative posture, one that is ready to receive the Lord.

The journey to Bethlehem has placed us on the road of God's promise, a prophetic promise that gives us hope. Reflect upon how this journey calls you to be contemplative, how we must take time to ponder. The journey to Bethlehem awakens in us the incarnate mystery that is Emmanuel— "God with us." Reflect upon the journeys in your life that have made you aware of God within you, not a text book image but the personal and intimate experience of God.

This happens because there is a birthing within, our allowing God to find a place within, but we must open up, we must trust the vulnerability this demands. There is a Holy card image that captures this and you may have seen it. Christ is standing at the door, but when we look closely we see the door has no knob stressing that we must open the door so the Lord may enter. The Journey to Bethlehem opens the heart to God. Our spiritual journey is about letting go of untruths about our deepest self. Think of what others may believe about you that you know are questionable. Own up to these and let go of what is untrue.

Mary's fiat, thy will be done, is a great help in reflecting on this journey. You may want to make up your own "to be list" and set aside the doing of your life. As you enter the stillness recall that the journey to Bethlehem began with the angel Gabriel's greeting Mary. Her openness is found in the prayer known as the "Hail Mary." Our Lady's response is worth reflecting upon as you ponder over today's journey, your journey to Bethlehem.

> Hail Mary, full of grace. The Lord is with you. Blessed are you among women and blessed is the fruit of thy womb, Jesus. Holy Mary, Mother of God, pray for us sinners, now and at the hour of our death. Amen.

# Chapter 2: Journey into Egypt:
## An Alien Road

*...flee to Egypt, and remain there till I tell you*

The journey to Egypt is an unexpected one that confronts evil in our life. It is an encounter with the uncertainties of life that we must face. These are the journeys that come in the spiritual night and compel us to confront the places within that were once places of bondage. Matthew tells us of the magi's' departure and Joseph's warning to flee, to journey yet again. Read Matthew 2:13–15.

The Escape to Egypt

13 Now after they had left, an angel of the Lord appeared to Joseph in a dream and said, "Get up, take the child and his mother, and flee to Egypt, and remain there until I tell you; for Herod is about to search for the child, to destroy him." 14 Then Joseph got up, took the child and his mother by night, and went to Egypt, 15 and remained there until the death of Herod. This was to fulfill what had been spoken by the Lord through the prophet, "Out of Egypt I have called my son." (*NRSVCE*)

Here I would like to explore a different kind of journey. These are the journeys that everyone must face and for some it is more intense, more spiritually demanding. As we know, the journey to Egypt is not one that has been planned, it is one that comes to us unwelcomed in the night hours and it demands of us both a taking leave, even a kind of fleeing, and it demands a trek into alien soil. For the Holy Family there was no easy comfort, no safe haven. They were forced to flee due to the murderous heart of Herod.

Dominicans, of which I am one, are dedicated to the truth, but hopefully that truth is kindly clothed in charity. So what I'm about to say may or may not apply to you but for many women and men there can be a spiritual "dark night of the soul" as John of the Cross so aptly named it. We can appear to others so solid but inside we struggle. Our flight into Egypt often is the encounter with evil that seems to torment us, and which we vainly try to hide or deny. We can easily find ourselves feeling abandoned, neglected, unloved and unlovable, that we take flight out into our desert, to that place of ancient bondage, the "Egypt" of our life – old hurts, insecurities, pride, envy, on and on. But spiritually speaking, Egypt is an alien land and a place of escape.

Perhaps no one individual has better helped me to know that even a good and holy person can experience this alien land than has Mother Teresa of Calcutta. The book *Come be My Light, the Private Writings of the Saint of Calcutta*[4] is powerful. The dedication reads "For those, especially the poorest of the poor, who find themselves in any form of darkness, that they may find in Mother Teresa's experience and faith, consolation and encouragement." I'm amazed at how many good people, who each day leave their homes feeling desperate, alone, isolated and no one seems to notice, no one seems to care. Listen to her own words: "I have no faith – I dare not utter the words and thoughts that crowd in my heart and make me suffer untold agony."(187)

The flight into Egypt is the flight of a broken heart, the accumulated hurts and unkindness that over time compel us to run, but where? Sadly we run to the safety of our false façades, what Mother Teresa describes as "a mask" or "a cloak that covers everything." Sadness and despair are no

---

[4] *Mother Teresa of Calcutta*, Brian Kolodiejchuk, M.C. ed. & comment. (New York: Doubleday, 2007).

strangers to even those most saintly among us. Even where we find good, we can see the flaws, the imperfections that linger around the good. I think it is fair to say that we live in an evil age, a time where we, like Herod, slaughter the holy innocents all over again, where we seek to destroy God and sink more deeply into evil. Just as we fear the darkness of that night, we must recall a dream, like Joseph's dream. Something in the dark of the night comes to us that holds a promise, for you see, the flight into Egypt is a divinely guided journey. Yes we flee in fear, anxious and hounded by death, but some small voice inside gives us comfort. It was an angel that gave Joseph a warning in the twilight awareness of a dream. In this divine guidance we, like Joseph, are free to move away from our fears of Herod, to the faith and courage of Joseph.

Years ago I gave a retreat for women religious in Michigan. In the evening I shared a book by Gary Chapman called, *The Five Love Languages*.[5] I commented how families were fortunate because they have psychologists and social workers studying family systems. I don't think that psychologists are brave enough to study the dynamics of religious community life. Regardless, Chapman had an insight as to how people express their love and register their being loved. I remember the five by GASTQ: G – Gifts, some people show their love by gifts, small little things, it's not the cost that counts but the giving that means so much; A – Affirmation, these are words of affirmation, letting one know they have value; S – Service, this is doing things for others because you know it means something to them, like making coffee in the morning even if you don't care for it; T – Touch,

---

[5] Gary Chapman, *The Five Love Languages: How to express Heartfelt Commitment to Your Mate* (Northfield Publishing: Chicago; 1995).

11

this is just a pat on the back, a hand on the shoulder, some human contact; Q – Quality Time, this is spending time with someone, not having to do anything, just being with them. After that session an elderly sister came to me with tears in her eyes confiding to me that all her time in the convent she didn't think she was loved, and now she realized that she was loved. She could see that there were other languages which she hadn't realized. Often times the flight into Egypt is one of a self-imposed loneliness that even we do not understand.

In order to face this loneliness we must recognize that the spiritual journey into Egypt is about two important realities: one is the child Jesus and the other is his mother, Mary. Joseph took both child and mother in the night and departed. This spiritual journey must always call us to the new born baby and the virgin mother. But what does this say to us about the inner life? Self-imposed loneliness will only be overcome in the vulnerability of birth and in the nurturing of maternal love. It tells us that in our dark nights, and our desperate hours, it is the vulnerability of a child that teaches us to cross the desert wilderness. So often we are afraid to risk, to let-go of all the things that hold us back. There is a risk in "letting go" even of our hurts. Over time it is the old hurts, the wounds we do not allow to heal that drag us away from God. We tend to guard our wounds, we try to protect them and so they fester. The lesson that Joseph shows us is that we must arise, take possession of our inner child and mother and depart. All too often we dwell upon our bitterness and fail to understand the miracle of mother and child, of care encountering another's needs, even our own. The anguish of childbirth must be set aside for new life to unfold. I think forgiveness, that is forgiving others their faults, is the epitome of a mother's love, regardless of gender.

St. Augustine in Sermon 19 tells us: "Let us never assume that if we live good lives we will be without sin; our lives should be praised only when we continue to beg for pardon. But men [*sic.*] are hopeless creatures, and the less they concentrate on their sins, the more interested they become in the sins of others. They seek to criticize, not to correct. Unable to excuse themselves, they are ready to accuse others" (*Office of Reading*, XIV Sunday Ordinary Time). True forgiveness arises from one's deep awareness of being forgiven.

The spiritual lesson of Mother and Child is one of learning, of teaching so that one is able to grow. If I might for a moment view this relation of the classic parent-child dynamic in arm-chair psychological terms. Often times it is our inner child that discloses to us our wounded-ness, this is the flight into Egypt. The adult work of dealing with psychological issues is part of the spiritual journey. Many times in houses of formation some of our young come to us with struggles from childhood, difficult home situations or traumatic events that they have over time suppressed. It really is the grace of the Holy Spirit that in the novitiate, seminary or even later, that the struggle surfaces and one can begin to journey, to heal. This is true in families, marriages and careers. Our inner parent, the self we hope to be, must, at these times, help our inner child come to face and hopefully grow into an adult faith. I know firsthand that sometimes this could take years. However, it is the blessing and the curse of our common life in Christ that we can either continue to dwell in exile or that we can see that "Herod" no longer lives, no longer holds us back. The spiritual journey into Egypt holds God's redemptive promise because this journey ultimately must take us out of Egypt, delivers us from the land of bondage into a land of promise.

## Take Time to Ponder

Here we come to the end of this day's journey and now take some time to ponder, or perhaps make some time to reflect on this journey in your life, its meaning for you. Taking time might seem hard to do but the choice is critical. Turn off the television, the radio, the computer and place yourself in a contemplative posture, receptive, open to hear God within. Take a few moments to reflect upon the wounds that have marked your journey, those hurts, sadness and aches. Examine them to see what yet needs healing, what inner hurts are you holding on to that you need to give to God? Ask yourself which love language do you most respond to and what are the love languages of those you love? What masks have hidden you away from the love and care of others. In prayer, turn to St. Joseph and his special care for both the child Jesus and our Mother Mary in their time of exile and their return from Egypt.

After you have spent some time being still, listening from within, ask yourself how your life has met and meets those journeys to alien lands. For those schooled by years of struggle this road will be all too familiar. For those still too young, those who fear admitting they are flawed, this journey holds perhaps the most valuable lesson of life. Over a hundred years ago, Pope Leo XIII, whose concern for the workers and the poor mark the Church's social teaching, composed a prayer to St. Joseph to be recited after the rosary. It reflects the importance of the family amid social chaos and uncertainty and reminds parents, especially fathers of their unique vocation and obligation. Although it isn't commonly recited today it seems to me a good prayer at any time, especially given the journeys upon an alien road.

Prayer to St. Joseph

To you, O blessed Joseph, do we come in our tribulation, and having implored the help of your most holy Spouse, we confidently invoke your patronage also.

Through that charity which bound you to the Immaculate Virgin Mother of God and through the paternal love with which you embraced the Child Jesus, we humbly beg you graciously to regard the inheritance which Jesus Christ has purchased by his Blood, and with your power and strength to aid us in our necessities.

O most watchful guardian of the Holy Family, defend the chosen children of Jesus Christ; O most loving father, ward off from us every contagion of error and corrupting influence; O our most mighty protector, be kind to us and from heaven assist us in our struggle with the power of darkness.

As once you rescued the Child Jesus from deadly peril, so now protect God's Holy Church from the snares of the enemy and from all adversity; shield, too, each one of us by your constant protection, so that, supported by your example and your aid, we may be able to live piously, to die in holiness, and to obtain eternal happiness in heaven. Amen.

WE WALK BY FAITH

# Chapter 3: Journey to Jericho: The Merciful Road.

*"Jesus, Son of David, have mercy on me!"*

In this journey Jesus heals a blind beggar and it is a story of mercy and forgiveness. Luke tells us in simple words the healing of a beggar on the roadside who only wishes to receive his sight. Read Luke 18:35–42.

Jesus Heals a Blind Beggar Near Jericho

35 As he approached Jericho, a blind man was sitting by the roadside begging. 36 When he heard a crowd going by, he asked what was happening. 37 They told him, "Jesus of Nazareth is passing by." 38 Then he shouted, "Jesus, Son of David, have mercy on me!" 39 Those who were in front sternly ordered him to be quiet; but he shouted even more loudly, "Son of David, have mercy on me!" 40 Jesus stood still and ordered the man to be brought to him; and when he came near, he asked him, 41 "What do you want me to do for you?" He said, "Lord, let me see again." 42 Jesus said to him, "Receive your sight; your faith has saved you." (*NRSVCE*)

Have you heard about the funeral for the wife of an elderly gentleman? Well, his wife's graveside service was just barely finished, when there was a massive clap of thunder, followed by a tremendous bolt of lightning, accompanied by even more thunder rumbling in the distance. The little, old man looked at the priest and calmly said, "Well, she's there." I recall a plaque given to one couple on their 25th wedding anniversary which said, "Marriages are made in heaven, but so are thunder and lightning."

Marriages, and much of life require mercy and forgiveness which is this journey's theme.

I would like us to explore this spiritual journey of new sight, a journey of forgiveness and mercy. How often in the spiritual life must we face our blindness, our failure to see what is present to us. You've heard the saying that one can't see the forest for the trees? Well many people today can't see the trees for the trees. People can focus so much on the little stuff, be so overwhelmed by the details, that not only do they miss the big picture but they can't even see the things right in front of them. I find this at times in the confessional when people seem more fundamentalist than Catholic in their theology because they only see their sins and miss God's grace.

This next topic may seem out of place to some but it is a serious concern for many people and needs to be addressed. In my ministry I have been struck by how many young people are all too frequently coming to confession with the exact same sin. By frequently I mean every 2 to 3 days. Now I am pleased that people are coming to confession, but I am alarmed by a certain pattern I see among some. Pornography is a kind of blindness that inflicts many people. This is so wide-spread that the American Bishops issued a pastoral statement entitled "*Create in Me a Clean Heart*" which deals with what many of these young people confess and struggle to remedy, pornography. The document doesn't dance around the issue:

> Given how widespread and easily accessible pornography is in today's society, everyone is vulnerable. Many people struggle with pornography use, including faithful Catholics, people of faith, people of no faith, married and single people, fathers and mothers, the young and the old, clergy and those in consecrated life. .... Pornography use is especially high

> among young adults, and it has been reported that the
> average age of first exposure to pornography is as early as
> eleven, with boys being more likely than girls to be exposed
> at an earlier age and to view more extreme content before
> the age of eighteen.[6]

I think that this topic is appropriately addressed in treating the Road to Jericho for it is a merciful road and merits serious treatment. Pornography is an epidemic and our prayers, especially for the young, are so needed. What I find challenging in this is how the gifts of sight and human sexuality have been so exploited creating a blindness of sorts. The media in particular has made us a culture of what I call "media-Platonist." By this I mean that they make us think that the image or the media is more real than the real. Porn isn't always of a sexual nature, violent video games, even social media can also distort a person's sense of reality. As Plato's analogy of the cave demonstrates, people see the media as reality, but these are shadows. More and more people think them real and fail to examine what is really real. St. Thomas Aquinas has helped me to ponder the Truth, to look for the really real. As it is said, "To know a thing rightly we must know it in its causes." Sadly for many people they look no further than the superficial veneer, the slick marketing, the shallow social media and the hollow political rhetoric. This is all as much a blindness as is having no sight at all, for "they have eyes but they do not see and ears but they do not hear" (Psalm 135:16). The challenge, it seems to me, is how do we help one another to see, how do we share the vision revealed in Christ? This is a genuine pastoral challenge.

---

[6] *Create in Me a Clean Heart: A Pastoral Response to Pornography* (Washington, DC; United States Conference of Catholic Bishops; 2015) p. 11.

One of my pastoral struggles when I went to do university chaplaincy was that the Sacrament of Reconciliation, which I love, had been turned into a sacrament of convenience. Like a fast food drive up, offering a quick relief but little or no nourishment. Sadly for some this convenience store mentality about confession created a "buyers-market Christian." They demanded the Church's ministry, but discarded it like the wrapper around their burger. They felt good, but it never fed the deeper hunger for true conversion. The pastoral concern is how to restore the power of true conversion to the sacrament of reconciliation, especially when people wrongly see the superficial as the real, the pornographic in place of the sacred. Such conversion demands a profound interior change in the person. The journey to Jericho teaches us that we must be beggars, we must stop at the roadside and really petition, really ask with all our hearts and souls to be forgiven. On the road to conversion begging is crucial, for a true beggar knows his needs, her wants, what is lacking. All the more so, a blind beggar lacks even the capacity to see.

A few years ago when I was living in England some dear friends came to visit and one day trip we took together was to see Stonehenge, that famous structure left by an ancient people. While it was truly fascinating we were distracted and our focus was drawn to another scene. Not far off in the surrounding meadows there were sheep grazing, which isn't uncommon in England, but all of us at the same moment were drawn to the same thing. One lamb appeared to be lifeless, its legs were pointed skyward, no movement, no sign of life at all, apparently dead. For the longest time we wondered if it was dead or not, our hearts feeling very sad for this lost little lamb. Then all of a sudden it leapt up to its feet darting to and fro amid the other sheep. Well I don't know how to explain it, perhaps my insane sense of humor, or perhaps some mysterious element found only at Stonehenge, but I began to channel what that lamb was saying, as she dashed to and fro so excitedly. For she had spent the last hour or so looking up at the clouds, the big blue sky, the bright sun, and suddenly she realized all the other sheep were missing this vision. She darted, so I imagined, shouting "Guys look up! Look up! It is so pretty! It's blue! I tell you, stop keeping your heads buried in the grass, feeding your belly, look up!

This story illustrates that blindness can be real, not because one has lost their sight but because one has lost their vision. All too often we keep our heads down, seeing only the food that fills our belly or gives us pleasure but we need to know that the vista of our vision grows more expansive the more we lift our sight. Look up!

There is another aspect of this blind beggar on the road to Jericho that teaches us a spiritual lesson. I imagine again the blind beggar sitting by the roadside and one day he is overwhelmed by the sound of a multitude going by. Where is everyone headed? Where are they coming from? There is a spiritual lesson in this Jericho journey. We must ponder our origin and our destiny, our beginning and our end. Life is a multitude of activity that passes by our roadside, the activities of our day. We need to attend to this passing parade of our days and listen to the good and the bad for the unexpected miracle worker who draws near.

We've all heard the saying that we learn from our mistakes, right? Well I'll tell you it's not true. We don't learn a single thing from our mistakes! We only learn from the mistakes we reflect upon. So too, like the blind beggar at the roadside of life we ponder our past, our present and our future and we must ask "what does it mean?" The journey to

Jericho is a moment of awareness, of profound conversion that realizes now, at this moment, our hope draws near. Hear the beggars cry "Jesus, son of David, have mercy on me!" which changes everything. Or does it?

Unfortunately, this first conversion is timid; it has within it a raw vulnerability. All too often those up in front, as it says, "rebuke us." You know the ones, those whom we think of as so perfect, the ones against whom we judge ourselves. I'm not good enough, or holy enough, or dedicated enough. How often do we find that we can be more unforgiving of our own selves than we are of others? Even when God has cast our sins far behind us we hold on to them. Like the blind beggar we need to be brave, end our second guessing and shout "Jesus, son of David, have mercy on me!" It is only at this moment that mature conversion of heart manifests itself, for we are brought to Jesus. I so wish for these young students, the ones who only see in the sacrament of reconciliation themselves as sinners, that they might one day realize the point of the sacrament is to meet Him, the shepherd whose love has redeemed us.

I recall a person who for years was weighed down by circumstances that happened when she was young. Physically her appearance was bent, burdened, she averted her eyes, avoided looking people in the face, all because she held on to the sin and the guilt that she couldn't let go of. One day I asked her if she enjoyed holding on to all the old hurts. I said it seems to me that you are trying to go on vacation, but you are packing your luggage with bricks. Now, personally I have learned over the years to cut in half what I think I need to pack. I was notorious for traveling with more than I needed. Things weigh us down, they hold us back! Dominican Fr. Allan White, the former provincial of the English province wisely observed "On most journeys we pack, but for the spiritual journey we must unpack." The journey to Jericho is a spiritual journey which brings us to encounter Christ, but more importantly, Christ confronts us with the question we must answer: "What do you want me to do for you?"

Here is the great miracle of the journey to Jericho, we are asked to name our greatest need, what is our greatest want. I wonder what went through the mind of the blind beggar when he heard that question. Fortune? Power? Fame? No, none of these but one simple request "Lord that I might see."

There is a video on the internet of a young man in his mid-20s with his father riding along in a train. The young man is looking out the window at the world passing by. Suddenly he shouts excitedly "Look dad the trees are going backwards!" His father smiled, a couple sitting nearby looked at the 24-year-old's childish behavior with pity. Then the boy shouted with joy "Dad, look the clouds are running with us!" The couple couldn't resist and said to the father, "Why don't you take your son to a good doctor?" The man smiled and said "I did. We are just coming from the hospital. My son was blind from birth; he just today has been given his vision."

Imagine what it might be like to see the world in a new way, to see the things we never even noticed. The journey to Jericho is about discovery, of realizing that even in our poverty, our sinfulness and blindness, faith still is working within: "Jesus, Son of David, have pity on me."

## Take Time to Ponder

As you take some time to ponder this journey I suggest you set a time and close your eyes and for ten minutes listen to all the sounds around you. Pay attention to where your thoughts go and the images that emerge. Resist the temptation to look, to open your eyes. Instead, imagine the beggar's struggle and reflect upon your own spiritual blindness. Ask yourself, "What in my life limits my vision, keeps me from looking up?" Allow yourself to echo the beggar's cry, "Jesus, Son of David, have mercy on me." In prayer repeat this simple plea as you hear in your heart the voice of Jesus asking you "What do you want from me?" Listen to your heart's petition on this journey to Jericho. What is your greatest need? Why?

For some of us whose years and life experiences have given an all too familiar relation with our sins, we beg. We have a sense that God knows us like the Samaritan woman at the well in John (4:4–42) whose faith rests on Christ truly knowing her, "he told me everything I have done" (v.39). For some of us sin looms about crushing the innocence we fear has been lost or sin tries to convince us that it really doesn't matter. This may be the most self-alienating lie, that I am guiltless, for it undermines personal integrity in a way that only we may know. It is this journey to Jericho that allows us to know from within our real needs, no matter the voices that try to hush us we cry out all the more.

The journey to Jericho meets the mercy of God and the reality of our deepest need. The sacrament of reconciliation is one place where the Jericho road takes sacramental form. Spend some time looking to God's mercy, the most authentic sign of love. One prayer I learned that helps me to see God's mercy is the act of contrition, learned when I was young but still vivid in my heart. I know that there have been various translations but the one I most cherish goes:

O my God, I am heartily sorry for having offended Thee, and I detest all my sins because of Thy just punishments, but most of all because they offend Thee, my God, Who art all-good and deserving of all my love. I firmly resolve, with the help of Thy grace, to sin no more and to avoid the near occasions of sin. Amen.

# Chapter 4: Journey to Jerusalem: The Savior's Road.

*...they were amazed, and those who followed were afraid*

This journey is a challenging one for it confronts the will of the Father and our struggle to understand it. There is a certain sense of poverty and obedience which are hallmarks of this journey. Mark writes of Jesus telling his disciples of his destiny, his passion, and yet they journey to Jerusalem. Read Mark 10:32–34.

> A Third Time Jesus Foretells His Death and Resurrection
>
> 32 They were on the road, going up to Jerusalem, and Jesus was walking ahead of them; they were amazed, and those who followed were afraid. He took the twelve aside again and began to tell them what was to happen to him, 33 saying, "See, we are going up to Jerusalem, and the Son of Man will be handed over to the chief priests and the scribes, and they will condemn him to death; then they will hand him over to the Gentiles; 34 they will mock him, and spit upon him, and flog him, and kill him; and after three days he will rise again." (*NRSVCE*)

This journey draws us into the reality of poverty and obedience. As professed religious know these two vows are significant in shaping their lives. Apostolic poverty, that sense of holding all things in common, demands a fuller sense of obedience and true obedience comes not from power but from poverty. The call to mendicant poverty isn't about denial but rather it is about dependency. Sometimes spiritual lessons translate from consecrated religious life to everyone living the Christian life. I recall in my novitiate year one of my brother novices, who is no longer with us, had a sense that poverty was destitution and that everyone else was not destitute enough. He prided himself on how he was living poverty, but the fact of the matter is he was a very stingy person.

Poverty that lacks generosity, no matter how meager our means, is a flawed understanding of poverty. True poverty frees us to be generous, not just with our treasures, but with our time and talents as well. Religious choose to be poor not as some Spartan badge of spiritual superiority, but to give witness. We all choose apostolic simplicity to allow our lack, our needs to be known, to place before the world our vulnerability, our need for them, for others whose charity and kindness blossom. For you see it is only in our surrendering ownership that we find that we are dependent. It is only out of the poverty of will, a surrender that I am called to truly obey, when I become obedient to the gracious gift of God. Now in saying this I will confess that the lived reality of professed obedience isn't so easy. It isn't always easy to surrender and trust, especially if trust is not the soil in which a person has been allowed to grow. I have heard from many religious women and men what I find to be horror stories because there was no trust, for too long the blistering heat of hurts made barren their soul's soil, so trust was a seed that could not and would not take root. One Dominican told me, on this issue of obedience that he was very fortunate because all his superiors were educable. I asked him what that meant, and he said, "I was able to re-teach them." Unfortunately, I've had some superiors who one might say were a bit less educable. My point is that both poverty and obedience require trust and the journey to Jerusalem helps us to discover what this means in our life.

That reminds me of a story. A man feared his wife wasn't hearing as well as she used to and he thought she might need a hearing aid. Not quite sure what to do, he called the family doctor who gave him a simple test. He said, "Stand about 40 feet away from her, and in a normal conversational speaking tone see if she hears you. If not, go to 30 feet, then 20 feet, and so on until you get a response." That evening, his wife was in the kitchen cooking dinner, and he was in the next room. He said to himself, "I'm about 40 feet away, let's see what happens." Then in a normal tone he asked, 'Honey, what's for dinner?" No response. So, he moved closer to the kitchen and repeated, "Honey, what's for dinner?" Still no response. Next, he moved into the dining room where he was about 20 feet from his wife and asked, "Honey, what's for dinner?" Again, he got no response. So, he walked up to the kitchen door, about 10 feet away. "Honey, what's for dinner?" Again, there is no response. So, he walked right up behind her. "Honey, what's for dinner?" "Herman, for the fifth time... CHICKEN!"

Often, we think the problem is theirs when it is really our own. Poverty and obedience complement one another. Only when we realize our lack, our need, can we obey, genuinely hear the will of God at work in our life. Now much was written, especially after World War II on duty and the danger of blind obedience. True obedience is never an excuse to forego the moral virtues, even religious superiors are bound by obedience to the rule of life and for many communities it is through the *vox capitulum*, the voice of the chapter. It is in this obedience that we discover both our abilities and our needs. A hallmark of the common life is the axiom: "from each according to her abilities, to each according to her needs." Both abilities and needs must always be assessed in light of truth and goodness. Honesty and charity seem to me to be the fruits of obedience and poverty, a community's genuineness and its generosity are found when we, like Herman in the story, realize the issue is our own. This, I confess, can be a life-long journey.

The passage we saw from Mark begins with a simple but important phrase "and they were on the road..." Being on the road, this *in via,* captures life and movement. When I first thought of these talks and using these stories of journeys I initially referred to them as being "on the road" until one friend asked if Bob Hope and Bing Crosby were anywhere in my talks. (A reference only a vintage crowd may recall.) Needless to say, "journey" became the focus but that does not take away from the reality of being *in via*, "on the road."

When I lived in part of Kansas which I found to be unexpectedly hilly, there was to my surprise a large wilderness area in the Flint Hills. It is one of the largest national prairie grass areas in the U.S., grasslands that the early settlers would have found. These grasses can grow to be 8 to 10 feet tall and the winds create beautiful waves of deep green. One Spring day I hiked one of the trails and these grasses were just beginning to grow, already about 1 to 2 feet. Everywhere there were all sorts of wildflowers, but the important thing I want to share is what it meant to be on foot, a pedestrian walking on the road. Of course, there was the initial excitement as you begin feeling this isn't that tough. At the beginning the road bends and crosses a stream. The path ambles through some woods on fairly level ground and then there was a slight rise as the trees almost formed a gateway. It was magical. As I reached the top of this enchanted portal I was confronted with a choice. Before me the road seemed to go on and on and on, in an almost direct ascent to the top of the high ridge. My first thought was I should just turn around and go back to the car. But pride told me to go on, as well as the sound of my doctor's exhortation to exercise. So I went on, passed by young fit hikers more often than not, but also noting those still far behind me, which encouraged me on. Once I reached the top, the trail turned and followed along the hill atop a ridge, the grass meadow on one side and the river valley on the other. I recall thinking "I feel like I could be hiking the Scottish Highlands." Yes I am a bit of a mad romantic. Then the road curved and began to descend. The heat of the day, the dust of the road made me again wonder if I was doing the right thing. My only consolation was that I told myself it was now probably shorter to go forward than to turn back.

The journey to Jerusalem is a journey of commitment, of obedience. It is one of going forward, of realizing that one's will must surrender to the ultimate end, the divine will of the Father. The disciples who walked the way with Jesus were confused. How could this man go to a place of such danger? They were afraid, but he continued on. There is something spiritually beneficial when we realize that faith is the antidote, the remedy to our fear. Gabriel's greeting to Mary at the Annunciation; the heavenly choir's greeting to the shepherds in the field, were both the same, "fear not." A person of faith is not foolishly fearless but rather knows that fear serves a purpose, it is not an end. Fear raises our awareness; it heightens our senses and it can either scare us away or empower us to carry-on. Cowardice and courage are both born out of fear. Again, it is at this moment that poverty and obedience confront us. Our fears about what Eckhart called *Nicht*[7] "the not," what we lack or don't have confront

---

[7] Meister Eckhart speaks of this in his *Book of Divine Consolation*, telling us that our unhappiness lies in our dwelling on what is lacking, what we do not have. This is not to be confused with John of the Cross's ascetical "nada" in the *Ascent of Mount Carmel*.

the obedience that tells us to do it, to obey. The journey to Jerusalem is one in which we know that ahead there is danger. Yet even though there is danger, from somewhere we encounter the small voice that calls us on. All of us know of the hesitancy and uncertainty that can paralyze us. I have great sympathy for those in leadership who have been entrusted with the common good of our future but must make decisions, almost always being second guessed, by well-meaning armchair experts. It is so much easier to acquiesce, to give in to the fears and uncertainty and cling to the *status quo*. His own disciples more or less said "Jesus, let's just turn back and spend our lives safely and quietly at home." Clearly the disciples harbored such doubts. However, Jesus doesn't turn back, he doesn't revert to the old, but instead he offers us the new, a new promise and new hope, our converting to the divine will of the Father.

I have to say that in this passage I take great comfort in how Jesus dealt with the fearful twelve disciples. He took them and spoke to them of what was ahead. Imagine what this meant to hear blow by blow of what was to come. It was the obedience of the Son to the divine will of the Father. Yes, but more, it was the ultimate voluntary poverty to surrender himself to sinful man. This *kenosis*, this self-emptying, is what the journey to Jerusalem teaches us. In the spiritual life the hardest journey is when we turn our feet to Jerusalem, the future that we fear. It can be an assignment by our superior, election to an office we don't know if we could handle or illness or aging, or uncertain financial futures, or a world that seems to have gone mad. The journey to Jerusalem is perhaps the most significant journey in this life, for it enables us to hear the voice of the Lord calling us to obey – "Thy will be done."

Allow me to finish my hiking story. The trail went on quite a bit further than I thought. I was tired and exhausted and just scarcely made it back before a rainstorm hit, and let me tell you storms in Kansas can be quite the experience. Like the journey to Jerusalem my hike has been better understood, more fully appreciated after it was done. These kinds of journeys are best appreciated in the past perfect tense of life, "to have had" for the present tense cannot do it justice. Reflecting upon life is the best way to reap its harvest. As Socrates said, "The unexamined life simply is not worth living."

## Take Time to Ponder

Here we come to the end of this journey. Now take a moment to review the fearful journeys in your own life, those times of challenge and change. For those of us who have been around, starting a new career, getting fired from a job, having to make a move, facing an illness, divorce, or death, all of these are part of the journey to Jerusalem. But the young too face this journey in the broken-heartedness of dating, in the sense of failure born of exams or dead-end careers. It is in this journey that obedience and dedication take shape. Think about it, it is a time of surrendering to the will of the Father. They are uncertain times but at the same instant they are about salvation and redemption. It is a journey of obedience to the Father. Jerusalem is the place of redemptive suffering, Golgotha and the empty tomb. Pay close attention to the fear that lingers in your heart: mockery that leaves us feeling demeaned; the dehumanizing sense of being spat upon; the searing pain of being flogged; or the ultimate annihilation of murder. Each of us, to varying degrees, knows these realities of the road to Jerusalem.

Allow your heart to face them, in poverty of soul and obedience of will, look within, for only the shroud is left if we obey the divine will.

As the disciples journeyed with Jesus facing their challenges they asked him how to pray. In response we see in Matthew's Gospel chapter 6 a prayer of poverty and obedience, of trust and mercy. The Our Father is the perfect prayer for the journey to Jerusalem:

> Our Father, Who art in Heaven, hallowed be Thy name; Thy Kingdom come, Thy will be done on earth as it is in Heaven. Give us this day our daily bread; and forgive us our trespasses as we forgive those who trespass against us; and lead us not into temptation, but deliver us from evil. Amen.

# Chapter 5: Journey to Emmaus:
# The Well-Traveled Road

*Did not our hearts burn within us while he talked to us on the road,...*

This is the journey of recognition and the sacramental presence in the breaking of the bread, for in the real and abiding presence of Christ we become a Eucharistic people and understand what true adoration means. Luke tells us of the uncertainty and confusion following the Lord's Passion through the experience of two disciples journeying to Emmaus. Read Luke 24:13–35.

### The Walk to Emmaus

13 Now on that same day two of them were going to a village called Emmaus, about seven miles from Jerusalem, 14 and talking with each other about all these things that had happened. 15 While they were talking and discussing, Jesus himself came near and went with them, 16 but their eyes were kept from recognizing him. 17 And he said to them, "What are you discussing with each other while you walk along?" They stood still, looking sad. 18 Then one of them, whose name was Cleopas, answered him, "Are you the only stranger in Jerusalem who does not know the things that have taken place there in these days?" 19 He asked them, "What things?" They replied, "The things about Jesus of Nazareth, who was a prophet mighty in deed and word before God and all the people, 20 and how our chief priests and leaders handed him over to be condemned to death and crucified him. 21 But we had hoped that he was the one to redeem Israel. Yes, and besides all this, it is now the third day since these things took place. 22 Moreover, some women of our group astounded us. They were at the tomb early this morning,

23 and when they did not find his body there, they came back and told us that they had indeed seen a vision of angels who said that he was alive. 24 Some of those who were with us went to the tomb and found it just as the women had said; but they did not see him." 25 Then he said to them, "Oh, how foolish you are, and how slow of heart to believe all that the prophets have declared! 26 Was it not necessary that the Messiah should suffer these things and then enter into his glory?" 27 Then beginning with Moses and all the prophets, he interpreted to them the things about himself in all the scriptures.

28 As they came near the village to which they were going, he walked ahead as if he were going on. 29 But they urged him strongly, saying, "Stay with us, because it is almost evening and the day is now nearly over." So he went in to stay with them. 30 When he was at the table with them, he took bread, blessed and broke it, and gave it to them. 31 Then their eyes were opened, and they recognized him; and he vanished from their sight. 32 They said to each other, "Were not our hearts burning within us while he was talking to us on the road, while he was opening the scriptures to us?" 33 That same hour they got up and returned to Jerusalem; and they found the eleven and their companions gathered together. 34 They were saying, "The Lord has risen indeed, and he has appeared to Simon!" 35 Then they told what had happened on the road, and how he had been made known to them in the breaking of the bread. (*NRSVCE*)

Without a doubt this story is one of my favorites in the New Testament because it captures so much of what the Christian life is meant to be. First, we are meant to be on journey, not to distant places but to those places within. Secondly, we are meant to talk with each other. Mature faith requires meaningful conversations. And thirdly it is about the things that happen in our life, God's abiding presence is the very mystery of existence as it unfolds and instructs us. *Deus est esse*, God is existence, beingness.

The Dominican Meister Eckhart captured this "beingness" in the German word he made up "*istikeit*" the is-ing of is-ness which is how I translate it. God is the underlying source of all that is. That is why we are able to ponder the mystery of creation itself and in this we see that the reality of Christ is made manifest. God talk, or theology, I confess is a Dominican's passion. But truth be told, Dominicans love to talk, after all our very name calls us to predicate, to name reality. However, the Emmaus journey instructs us in the nature of our conversation which must always be centered in the presence of Christ. We might not always recognize this, but in our genuine conversations we are attentive to one another and we reveal ourselves in our conversation. Conversation is a form of preaching and as I like to say *praedicamus et praedicamur*, we preach and our life is preached. Our doing, our conversing is both active, a doing, and passive, a being done. Conversation like conversion is a kind of turning over in which we encounter the presence of Christ in our midst, acting in our life. From 1986 to 1991 I studied in Louvain, Belgium and made some friends with my fellow doctoral students. I was the only one in our group doing dogmatic theology, two were in Scriptures and two were in moral theology. I recall a number of occasions just enjoying good conversation over a cup of coffee, sometimes something a bit stronger. Recall the adage "*in vino veritas*" well good theology has many wine stewards and cellarers. Conversations about faith are always formative. St. Dominic wisely advised his followers "to speak either to God or about God."

There are two things in Jesus' question to the travelers that strike me as noteworthy. One is that it engages one with the other, and the other noteworthy bit is that it is "on the way." Notice that they are stopped in their places and they are overwhelmed with sadness because they could not believe that this stranger was ignorant of the event that captured their minds and hearts. Their amazement leads them to engage the stranger asking, "Do you not know?"

The journey to Emmaus is our realizing the depths of the things that happen in our life. It is so typically Dominican to ground this journey in knowing, in understanding. As we understand these things we are drawn to the center of Christ, the humanity of Jesus Christ, his prophetic mission, his words and deeds, his messianic suffering, passion, death and resurrection. This knowledge is anchored to hope in a new life, the mystery of the Risen Lord. Here we encounter the journey's turn from puzzlement to belief, from our foolish ways to the ways of faith. Allow me to recall this one passage. In verses 25–31, Jesus confronts their superficial faith and delves into the meaning of the prophetic Scriptures on the Messiah. Just as they near the village they invite the stranger in and share with him at table. It is in this Eucharistic moment that their superficial faith gives way to the presence of the Risen Lord. It changes them forever.

The Emmaus journey, our genuine encounter with one another, brings us to knowing Christ in the Eucharist, his true and abiding presence. He is the stranger in our midst, who seems to be set to journey on. The Risen Lord completes four actions that enable us to see: he took, blessed, broke, and gave. This Eucharistic action shapes a fuller understanding of our Christian vocation as well. As a Dominican, my spirituality is ordered to Truth, but not the sterility of scientific truth, no, Dominican truth is disclosing, revealing what is beyond. It is the metaphysics of Faith, our going beyond the physical plane and seeing what is more than meets the eye. In thinking, we strive to intellectually grasp what is present. Study and prayer go hand in hand, for this is how we acquire—that is, our receiving the Lord. We must first appropriate the object, hold it, sense it, so that we can receive it and be blessed. Like Jacob, we wrestle with the divine truth, we take hold of it, wrestling through the night until daybreak. It is in the dawn hours that we find blessing (see Genesis 32:22–31).

The Eucharistic blessing is so abundant, so plentiful, that of its very nature it breaks into pieces, so as to be given. Over the years I have come to appreciate more and more that it isn't our perfections wherein God's mystery unfolds but more often in our flaws, our brokenness, our imperfections. True love isn't won because we found the perfect person. There is the story of the man wandering around in a field, thinking about how good his wife had been to him and how fortunate he was to have her. He asked God, "Why did you make her so kind-hearted?" The Lord responded, "So you could love her, my son." "Why did you make her so good-looking?" "So you could love her, my son." "Why did you make her such a good cook?" "So you could love her, my son." The man thought about this. Then he said, "I don't mean to seem ungrateful or anything, but ... why did you make her so dumb?" God replied, "So she could love you, my son."

The brokenness we find in the Eucharist is the source of our fullest meaning, our being given to others, the wounds by which we are healed. The Eucharist is the supreme encounter with imperfection's lovability, it is the embrace of our broken humanity and God's infinite love. Vatican II speaks of the Eucharist as "source and summit" (*Lumen Gentium* 11) for it is our encounter with Christ in whose wounds we have our redemption. In the bread blessed, broken and shared we encounter the saving mystery, in our common brokenness we find healing. It is in our journey with the stranger in our midst which allows us to see, that sets our hearts off eager to be shared.

I used to wonder just why Eucharistic adoration means so much to many of our young students nowadays. There is a surprisingly strong devotion among many of them. In one of my assignments we would have exposition once a week with 24 hours of adoration concluding with benediction. It is both thanksgiving (*eucharistia*) and prayer (*ad oratio*). Now let me remind you that these were college students with class schedules and busy social lives and yet they regularly committed for the entire semester to an hour of Eucharistic adoration. In addition, daily Mass on Tuesday, Wednesday and Thursday was at 9:30 pm! Yes, in the middle of the night, or so it seemed to me. For most of the year we would have 100 to 150 students each night. It is very impressive to see how many young people are looking to find this Emmaus encounter. For in today's world we can spend so much time chatting on line or texting by phone, but we miss the real encounter with the other, Christ in our midst. I pray for this younger generation who are growing up in a world of *faux* social interaction, of superficial media. They mistrust political institutions and perhaps rightfully so. Is there any wonder why they find such comfort and consolation in Eucharistic adoration? It is a true and abiding presence, something real and genuine. So too for us, the Emmaus journey must bring us to the Eucharist as the source and summit of our life. The Mass, time in chapel before the Blessed Sacrament, or an hour's devotion, all open our eyes to the presence of the Emmaus traveler who instructs our hearts and reveals the Sacred Scriptures. The Emmaus journey brings us to the resurrection, to new life, new hope, and new possibilities. The danger I see for some is an idolatrous misuse of Eucharistic adoration as a personal prop or crutch for one to feel good about being Catholic. Eucharistic adoration must always return one to the altar of sacrifice and the Eucharistic assembly, the Body of Christ in serving and caring for those in need. If not, the two disciples would have stayed in Emmaus contented and pleased with their experience. The journey to Emmaus is a sending forth from Emmaus to encounter the living Lord in our world, an acting and a being acted upon.

## Take Time to Ponder

Pause for a moment and think of the times of confusion and uncertainty in your life. Here no matter if you are young or old we all know such times. It may have been a struggle of faith, a life decision with no clarity, or a personal challenge about self-identity. Now ask yourself where on the Emmaus road do you encounter God, begin to realize your life's meaning? Do you find him in the questions of the day's topics you discuss, in the burning heart that finds new understanding, in the breaking of bread at the table, in the absence? Or, have you run from the stranger and continue to face the same struggle time and time again? The remarkable thing about the Emmaus journey is that we must invite the stranger in, open ourselves to a level of trust and vulnerability if we hope to recognize new life resurrected in Christ. The Emmaus journey is Eucharistic, for we come to realize who we are in relationship to who He is. It is a vanishing awareness that recognizes something burning within our very souls. What began in confusion ends in trust and returns us to Jerusalem, that place of Redemption.

41

On the Emmaus journey, this Eucharistic journey is worth reflecting on the great Eucharistic prayer of the Church. Notice that each begins with a familiar scripted dialogue of sorts between the presider and the assembly. This dialogue bestows blessing, hope, and gratitude. It is the journey to Emmaus that brings us back to Jerusalem. This simple exchange can be overlooked so it is important for us to ponder its meaning, to see the Emmaus stranger calling us to the Eucharistic mystery:

> The Lord be with you. *And with your Spirit.*
>
> Lift up your hearts. *We lift them up to the Lord.*
>
> Let us give thanks to the Lord, our God. *It is right and just.*

Even the end of Mass is a scripted dialogue bestowing blessing and mission:

> The Lord be with you. *And with your Spirit.*
>
> May almighty God bless you, the Father, and the Son, and the Holy Spirit. *Amen.*
>
> Go and announce the Gospel of the Lord. *Thanks be to God.*

# Chapter 6: Journey to Damascus: The Repentant Road

*"Saul, Saul, why do you persecute me?"*

On this journey we confront the false self, the self-righteous self that is so sure, so willed to do the will of God as we have defined it quite apart from God. This journey happens more often than we might want to admit. It is a journey of conversion and a change in our way of thinking and living. We read in the Acts of the Apostles how Saul set out to arrest and punish the followers of "The Way." As he traveled to Damascus he is struck blind and encounters the voice of the Lord accusing him of persecuting the Lord. In order to find healing Saul must seek out Ananias one of those people Saul was seeking to destroy. This enemy, Ananias must welcome and heal, even amid the fears. In the end Saul is baptized and becomes a believer, confounding even the Jews. Read Acts 9:1–22.

The Conversion of Saul

1 Meanwhile Saul, still breathing threats and murder against the disciples of the Lord, went to the high priest 2 and asked him for letters to the synagogues at Damascus, so that if he found any who belonged to the Way, men or women, he might bring them bound to Jerusalem. 3 Now as he was going along and approaching Damascus, suddenly a light from heaven flashed around him. 4 He fell to the ground and heard a voice saying to him, "Saul, Saul, why do you persecute me?" 5 He asked, "Who are you, Lord?" The reply came, "I am Jesus, whom you are persecuting. 6 But get up and enter the city, and you will be told what you are to do." 7 The men who were traveling with him stood speechless because they heard the voice

but saw no one. 8 Saul got up from the ground, and though his eyes were open, he could see nothing; so they led him by the hand and brought him into Damascus. 9 For three days he was without sight, and neither ate nor drank.

10 Now there was a disciple in Damascus named Ananias. The Lord said to him in a vision, "Ananias." He answered, "Here I am, Lord." 11 The Lord said to him, "Get up and go to the street called Straight, and at the house of Judas look for a man of Tarsus named Saul. At this moment he is praying, 12 and he has seen in a vision a man named Ananias come in and lay his hands on him so that he might regain his sight." 13 But Ananias answered, "Lord, I have heard from many about this man, how much evil he has done to your saints in Jerusalem; 14 and here he has authority from the chief priests to bind all who invoke your name." 15 But the Lord said to him, "Go, for he is an instrument whom I have chosen to bring my name before Gentiles and kings and before the people of Israel; 16 I myself will show him how much he must suffer for the sake of my name." 17 So Ananias went and entered the house. He laid his hands on Saul and said, "Brother Saul, the Lord Jesus, who appeared to you on your way here, has sent me so that you may regain your sight and be filled with the Holy Spirit." 18 And immediately something like scales fell from his eyes, and his sight was restored. Then he got up and was baptized, 19 and after taking some food, he regained his strength. For several days he was with the disciples in Damascus, 20 and immediately he began to proclaim Jesus in the synagogues, saying, "He is the Son of God." 21 All who heard him were amazed and said, "Is not this the man who made havoc in Jerusalem among those who invoked this name? And has he not come here for the purpose of bringing them bound before the chief priests?" 22 Saul became increasingly more powerful and confounded the Jews who lived in Damascus by proving that Jesus was the Messiah. (*NRSVCE*)

Now we travel to Damascus but more, it is a journey that confronts our false self, exposing our disordered self and breaks us down so as to be raised up. This journey I find the most challenging but strangely the most desired. The English poet John Donne beautifully captures it in his *Holy Sonnet 14* when he writes: "Batter my heart three-person'd God; for you as yet but knock, breathe, shine, and seek to mend..." or St. Augustine who declares in Book I of his *Confessions* "Our hearts are restless until they rest in Thee O Lord...." All the great spiritual writers have confronted this battle against the barriers that keep us back, keep us selfishly centered upon our own egos.

At this point I will speak only for myself but I trust that I am not alone. Henry Nouwen wisely said: "We like to make a distinction between our private and public lives and say, 'Whatever I do in my private life is nobody else's business.' But anyone trying to live a spiritual life will soon discover that the most personal is the most universal, the most hidden is the most public, and the most solitary is the most communal. What we live in the most intimate places of our beings is not just for us but for all people. That is why our inner lives are lives for others. That is why our solitude is a gift to our community, and that is why our most secret thoughts affect our common life." [8] So together we journey to Damascus.

To be honest, as much as I try not to, I find myself astride my prideful horse like Paul riding off to the synagogues of Damascus in order to make things right, to correct, to admonish. I can feel so justified in this that it is very difficult to see it any other way. "I'm helping these people and this is

---

[8] Henri Nouwen *Bread for the Journey: A Daybook of Wisdom and Faith* (San Francisco: Harper; 1997) 2:23

what God wants me to do." I tell myself this is what I would want someone to do if I were wrong and so I gallop on along this road to Damascus with a mission and purpose. More than once have I been thrown down and I confess the getting up has not been easy. As religious people we aspire to such noble purpose that our aspirations sometimes eclipse the more important realities. Allow me to share two stories.

I know a person who throughout his life has genuinely sought to serve, to feel as though his gifts were recognized and put to use by his community. But time and time again he felt discounted. Now I know that this is fairly true because I know that he was appreciated outside his community but as it says in the scripture "he came to his own and they received him not." Over the years, I have seen how he has slowly come to accept the fact that his part to play in things will be but a small one. I am heartbroken when I hear him speak about the inner struggle this has caused throughout his life. I can't help but wonder if Paul didn't struggle as well, to find out that the role he thought was his as a great defender of the Old Law of his ancestors was not the role intended by God.

Another person I know is a 100-year-old woman, and up until about six months ago she was living in her home where she brought up her children. She drove her somewhat dented car to church, grocery store, and her hairdresser. Her struggle now is one of letting go and my heart aches when I hear her speak about the pain of aging, no longer having the friends around from of old, of missing children and grandchildren and great grandchildren who now live all across the nation. This diminishment, this feeling she has of having lived too long is a struggle for her. She's a very prayerful woman and though she may from time to time lose her patience, I can see the slow and steady ways in which God is courting her, helping her to let go and fall into his embrace. It is this journey to Damascus wherein Saul had to trust and in turn to be trusted. That is the most difficult road to travel, to journey in order to rediscover the same "self" but on a different path than you had thought.

Back to Saul in our passage: When we read that he was "... still breathing threats and murder against the disciples of the Lord ..." I can't help but think of where we as a nation and our world have seemingly come to find ourselves. In a certain sense the story of Saul is emblematic of the world today. Anger is an emotion that so easily corrupts and distorts the human spirit. In both of the stories I recounted, hurt is the demon dragging both people down, a sense of injustice. One of the easiest ways for an operative to persuade an audience or stir up the crowd is to appeal to their emotions, and the volatile emotions are the easiest to inflame, even the smallest embers can be set ablaze. But why do these embers seem to smolder and are they never ending?

For this I turn to St. Thomas Aquinas and his tract on the emotions (*ST* I–II q. 22–48). If I might summarize and simplify, he wisely tells us that all of our emotions are given to us for a purpose and our error is that we use them wrongly. In particular when Thomas treats anger he tells us that anger rises due to a perceived injustice, either to my person or my property. So anger always has its origins in the perception of injustice. How primordial is this emotion and how often does it lead to violence which is an abuse of it? The spiritual journey to Damascus is often upon an angry road because it embodies all the injustices, real or perceived that we have known in our life. It is so easy to allow these injustices to fester into a fatal and violent passion "still breathing threats and murder." The danger is that like Saul we continue on the road of anger not realizing how distorted we become with every step. Our egos assure us that we are right, that they are wrong, and when we are done, everyone will realize how virtuous and righteous we are. But our ego hasn't allowed for one important thing—the destiny that God has in store for us.

On our journey to Damascus we are always going to be struck low by a light that shines upon our dim egos and confronts us with the truth. By name Saul was called and confronted with the reality that he would have never imagined – "why do you persecute me?" He had to recognize a power and authority greater than himself and asked "Lord" but still he did not know who it was that challenged him.

How often in our lives do we struggle with criticism, with challenges and simply want to know where this is coming from, who could say such things? It makes a world of difference once we know on what authority these charges are made. I wish that it were clearer. It would be great if more often the voice clearly responded, "I am Jesus." It would make things so much easier. But it is the next bit that is difficult for Saul and for us, when we hear the charge: "I am Jesus, whom you are persecuting."

I vividly recall years ago when I was a novice and in spiritual direction my director seemingly out of the blue asked me "Why are you afraid to let God love you?" I was stopped dead in my tracks. The question seemed absurd, of course I wanted God to love me, but I learned it was on my terms. I had my expectation of what that love would look like, and it didn't look like my not being in control. Suddenly I had a sense of why we speak of "falling in love" and not "deciding to love." Since then my love affair with God has been more like a river ride, I am carried by the current of His will. Oh don't get me wrong, I often fight, but I have learned that when I lock horns with God I know who is going to win in the end. It has taken me years to realize that I don't always do or go to the places I want to be, but I see now, that I have always ended up where I should have been. Slowly we discern what God is calling us to do, what God has in store for us.

There is another lesson in this journey to Damascus that we as adults need to learn, it isn't always our companions, those traveling with us, who comprehend the realities that change us. More often than not it demands of us a new destiny, not the same one we set out upon, but now perhaps seen in a new light to which we remain blind. It is not an easy thing to be led, to go somewhere that we cannot see. Our instincts and inclinations are to chart our own trail, to be the masters of our own destiny.

A few years back when my mom was a young 80 I noticed something I was doing to her, that I did not realize. I thought I was helping but clearly I was not. I would take her by the arm and guide her along the way. What I failed to realize is that she wanted to look around, to see what was going on, and to go where she wanted to go. Needless to say we were both frustrated in our plans, one wanting to control and the other not wanting to be controlled. Once I realized it was a no-win situation I did my best to be there for her, just to hold on to, that was what she needed most.

Fundamentally it is not easy to trust the guidance of others. This can be true in community life, family life or in parish ministry. How often must it be that the other person is the sighted one and we are left to trust their guidance? We are like Saul led away, our mistrust curbs our every step and we are tempted to resist, to rebel. Saul's way to master this temptation was to fast from food and drink, and these are helpful tools.

But the journey to Damascus tells us of another reality that is no less a part of the spiritual life, for it is also about the call of Ananias (and the Damascus community) as well as Paul. Realize that both sides, in their own way had to confront the destiny of their own design and surrender to God's plan for each. Ananias received his call in a vision while Saul's call was born of his loss of vision. Imagine Ananias' horror when he was told to trust his enemy. Ananias had fallen victim to the plague of many, the gossip and prejudice that we human beings trade in. It isn't easy not to be negative of our so-called enemies. We would feel justified in questioning and doubting a vision that told us to help our foes, and we'd be considered a fool to take in a terrorist, yet that is what Saul was. Still Ananias was such a fool, he trusted God's call despite his fears. Both men, Saul and Ananias underwent a conversion of sorts. As Christians our life only works where there is this spirit of mutual conversion. I know this sounds naïve and in my gut I cringe as I foresee the consequences. It isn't easy to let go and to allow the years gone by to be a thing of the past. But this is not solely our doing, we must open to the divine reality, the spirit at work in our midst. Imagine what Saul would have become had the Damascus community not risked. Chances are that he would not have been changed, for true conversion is a communal reality incorporating us into the Body of Christ. We ought not to underestimate Damascus, the community's role in God's plan.

Oddly the journey to Damascus is a journey of renewal. It nourishes us and strengthens us. But we must first shed the scales of our pettiness and stubbornness; they must fall from our eyes and hearts for they are prickly and poisonous things. It takes time, so we ought not to fall prey to a facile and easy fix. There must be a time where life is shared, where trust is built. It may never be perfect, and we may utter in amazement, "Aren't you the one who wreaked havoc here?" The bottom line is that we fail in learning the lesson of the journey to Damascus if we abandon the proof that demonstrates, by our words and deeds, the real presence of Christ. The journey to Damascus is about our intimate and personal relationship with Jesus, and to one another in Christ. There comes a point where we stop being Saul and are now called Paul.

## Take Time to Ponder

Here we come to the end of this journey and now take some time to ponder, to reflect on this journey in your life, its meaning for you. This is a journey that requires multiple perspectives, seemingly opposing views of our world. Saul's view was opposed to Ananias and vice versa. It doesn't take a sociologist to see that we live in a world of opposing views, but one in particular is worth reflecting upon. There is perhaps a genetic opposition between the idealism of the young and the realism of our elders. We can all too easily fixate on the particulars of my experience, my reality, that we box ourselves in and can only think in oppositional terms. The road to Damascus confronts this oppositional thinking and bids us to think relationally.

If you are honest with yourself, what is the conversion you fear the most? The road to Damascus is an avenue of angers and hurts. What wounds plague you, hold you back? Try to see yourself as Saul, deprived of vision and now try to see yourself as Ananias given a vision that demands trust. What lessons touch your heart? This journey to Damascus redefines us, calls us by a new name. Take note of how this conversion transforms and changes you, draws you into that divine image God has called you to be. Can you let go of the old?

As you ponder this journey of encounter I recommend you turn to the prayer associated with St. Francis of Assisi (c. 1182–1226). It is a beautiful prayer that calls us away from opposition to relation, from isolation to communion, from suspicion to trust:

> Lord, make me an instrument of your peace:
> where there is hatred, let me sow love;
> where there is injury, pardon;
> where there is doubt, faith;
> where there is despair, hope;
> where there is darkness, light;
> where there is sadness, joy.
>
> O divine Master, grant that I may not so much seek
> to be consoled as to console,
> to be understood as to understand,
> to be loved as to love.
> For it is in giving that we receive,
> it is in pardoning that we are pardoned,
> and it is in dying that we are born to eternal life.
> Amen.

# Chapter 7: Journey to Gaza: The Desert Road.

*"How can I, unless someone guides me?"*

On this our final journey we meet the Ethiopian Eunuch and the Apostle Philip who together capture the journey that every Christian must take, that of learning the Faith in a way wherein it becomes real. What does this mean? It is the difference between "knowing about" and "being familiar with."[9] In the spiritual life we can speak of this as study and prayer, of the mind's encounter with Truth and the heart's intimacy with the source of Truth. Let's see what the Acts of the Apostles tell us about this journey. We see that Philip is prompted by an angel to journey to Gaza, out into the desert. As he journeys he encounters an Ethiopian eunuch trying to understand the prophecy. Enlightened by the Spirit, Philip instructs the man who is baptized. Read Acts 8:26–40.

Philip and the Ethiopian Eunuch

26 Then an angel of the Lord said to Philip, "Get up and go toward the south to the road that goes down from Jerusalem to Gaza." (This is a wilderness road.) 27 So he got up and went. Now there was an Ethiopian eunuch, a court official of the Candace, queen of the Ethiopians, in charge of her entire treasury. He had come to Jerusalem to worship 28 and was returning home; seated in his chariot, he was reading the prophet Isaiah. 29 Then the Spirit said to Philip, "Go over to this chariot and join it." 30 So Philip ran up to it and heard him reading the prophet Isaiah. He

---

[9] The English language uses *to know* for both facts and people, but the French, German and Spanish languages, to name a few, have words for each. One verb expressing knowledge about facts or learned skills and another expressing familiarity or acquaintance with a person or place.

asked, "Do you understand what you are reading?" 31 He replied, "How can I, unless someone guides me?" And he invited Philip to get in and sit beside him. 32 Now the passage of the scripture that he was reading was this: *"Like a sheep he was led to the slaughter, and like a lamb silent before its shearer, so he does not open his mouth. 33 In his humiliation justice was denied him. Who can describe his generation? For his life is taken away from the earth."* 34 The eunuch asked Philip, "About whom, may I ask you, does the prophet say this, about himself or about someone else?" 35 Then Philip began to speak, and starting with this scripture, he proclaimed to him the good news about Jesus. 36 As they were going along the road, they came to some water; and the eunuch said, "Look, here is water! What is to prevent me from being baptized?" 38 He commanded the chariot to stop, and both of them, Philip and the eunuch, went down into the water, and Philip baptized him. 39 When they came up out of the water, the Spirit of the Lord snatched Philip away; the eunuch saw him no more, and went on his way rejoicing. 40 But Philip found himself at Azotus, and as he was passing through the region, he proclaimed the good news to all the towns until he came to Caesarea. (*NRSVCE*)

In this final journey we see similarities to the encounter on the road to Emmaus and of instruction that we saw on the road to Damascus. Here I wish to explore the themes of study and prayer in our lives, and the journey to Gaza as the desert road of learning. This story beautifully demonstrates the importance of instruction and understanding in adult faith, captured in the figures of Philip and the Ethiopian eunuch.

Years ago when I was assigned to Albuquerque my ministry was centered on Adult Faith Formation. I worked to establish the Dominican Ecclesial Institute (or D+E+I), but I also taught during the fall semester at the University of New Mexico. I was very fortunate to meet adult learners both in the formality of the classroom and in the freeness of personal enrichment classes. But both groups of people shared the same desire, they wanted to understand, some more eagerly than others. I recall one occasion with a group of about 30 people running in age from 30 to 70-ish, when after one personal enrichment class, an older gentleman almost dumbfounded commented "Why didn't anybody tell me this before?" Of course, in the back of my mind I was thinking, "Where have you been these last 30 years? Have you never read a book on Vatican II? Have you not participated in RCIA as a sponsor, or attended any of the hundreds of diocesan and parish offerings?" These were my thoughts, but at the same time I had a certain sadness realizing that for many Catholics they have settled for just a small bit of what their Faith is all about. They have sampled the petite *hors d'oeuvre*, but skipped out on the main meal. It is a genuine sadness for me to encounter so many Catholics, even members of my own family, who have settled for a Catholic-lite which is more fiction than fact. This journey to Gaza requires us to leave the safety and familiarity of Jerusalem and we, like Philip, must rise and travel south, which is a metaphor for the unknown. There is something stark about this journey, for the Scripture text specifically states: "This is a desert road."

There is a story of a person getting away from the cold winter. A man from Canada departed for his vacation in Miami Beach, where he and his wife were to meet the next day at the conclusion of her business trip to Chicago. They were both longing for the warm weather and some relaxing time together. Unfortunately, there was a problem at the boarding gate, and the man was delayed and put on a later flight. He complained to the agent but was told there was nothing they could do. Once he arrived at the hotel the next day, he found that Florida was having a heat wave. The hotel clerk gave him a message that his wife would arrive as planned. He could hardly wait to get into the pool and cool off, so he quickly sent his wife an email, but due to his haste he made an error in the address. His message arrived on the screen of an elderly woman whose even older husband had died the day before. When the grieving widow opened her email, she took one look at the monitor, let out an anguished scream, and fell to the floor. Her family rushed to the room where they saw this message on the screen: Dearest wife, departed yesterday as you know. Just now got checked in, some confusion at the gate. Appeal was denied. I received confirmation of your arrival tomorrow, your loving husband. P.S. Things are not as we thought. You're going to be surprised at how hot it is down here.

Sometime our travels are taken with unexpected journeyers and we arrive at unexpected destinations. For many people the desert is a hostile place, that is if we think life is only found amid lush greenery. When I was newly ordained my first assignment was to teach and do campus ministry in Grand Rapids, Michigan. Now I'm from the southwest, so it was challenging to face the winters up north, the dark and the cold. What depressed me even more was how little these Northerners knew or understood of my home, especially of the desert. Yes, the desert seems barren, but it is not lifeless. This is important for us to appreciate, especially as we spiritually journey to Gaza. The other thing is that in the Spring, the desert is a place of delicate beauty. Again, in the spiritual life, it is God's gentle and delicate presence that bestows the greatest grace. So like Philip, we go, heading south from fertile fields to what seems a barren land. But this barrenness is now embodied in a man, the eunuch. How often do we fail to see the person behind the barrenness, to see beyond one another's limitations? Yes, he is made barren by mutilation, or by fate, but at the same time this Ethiopian eunuch is one who is socially and perhaps politically laden with rank and privilege, even though as a man he is less so. Like Sara or Elizabeth, what was thought to be barren has life. This captures for us a spiritual sense of the human mind and heart which lacks both knowledge and love, such a person is incomplete. The significant point is not who this man was, though by external accounts we may judge him lacking, but more importantly the issue is who Philip encounters, the person the eunuch is striving to be.

Philip represents study and the eunuch prayer. Education is a leading forth, calling the mind from what it is not to become what it is meant to be. And so this eunuch of great social privilege traveled in relative luxury pondering the prophecies of Isaiah. It is here that study (the apostle Phillip) challenges the man's comprehension. "Do you understand what you are reading?" Now prayer (the eunuch) realizes that he must be guided. The fact of the matter is that study enriches prayer, and prayer enlivens study. In Dominican life there are four great pillars that balance our life and two of these are prayer and study. One without the other is only partial and they contribute to our common life and mission, which are the other two pillars. I say this because it has value for every Christian life as well.

So allow me to explore Dominican prayer and study. First it needs to be said that they are two sides of the same coin. In prayer our hearts and minds are raised to God, and in study we come to love the good and know the true. For the ancients the two faculties of the soul were our knowing and our loving. If we fail to keep these two aspects related, then we run the risk of either an elitist intellectualism or a shallow form of piety. This doesn't mean that we must be

57

some kind of cross between Einstein and a recluse. But that we should be thoughtful in prayer and prayerful in thought. What do I mean by that? Prayer and study are like the two wings of a great bird, both are necessary for flight and one without the other is doomed. Or again, just as we require our two eyes to be able to perceive depth and distance, so too study and prayer enhance our vision. This is a challenge for us all.

Now don't be too harsh on yourself for not being perfect. I always take comfort in the apostles that Jesus chose. Each one of them managed to get it not quite right, and Peter most of all. I think that the apostles give us hope that even with our limitations God is able to bend us toward His will. This journey to Gaza is one of discovery, of realizing how in pondering the Word of God in study and allowing our hearts to give voice in prayer, we are changed. Blaise Paschal (1623–1662), the French philosopher observed that, "the heart has reason that reason cannot understand," or the Dominican Jordan of Saxony (c. 1190–1237) who spoke of "the humble intelligence of the heart." Prayer and study are coupled because they seep into the crevices of our fullest humanity, our knowing and our loving. Together they have the power to complete our grasp on this world's wonders.

Like Philip in the passage from Acts, our understanding must run to catch the chariot of prayer. And prayer, like that eunuch, must invite study to guide and sit alongside prayer. The liturgy of the hours is a perfect example of this journey of prayer and study, for although we recite the psalms in prayer we are instructed in their meaning. Time and time again we hear the text and we are guided, instructed and formed by them. In the Office of Readings and in the Scriptures given in each hour, we study the lessons that are inspired by patristic writers, saints and church councils. Just as the eunuch asked what the passage of Isaiah meant, of whom does it speak, and just as Philip explained the good news of Jesus, so too do we in study and prayer find and follow Christ. Notice how it is that when prayer and study sit with one another, as did Philip and the eunuch, then something amazing happens—one is brought to new life in baptism. Notice that both men went into the water and when they came out of the water Philip was taken up, as though to say that study must always leave prayer in the waters of faith. Believing now no longer is in need of study, prayer is able to truly rejoice in the Lord. Study must move on to new towns, search new areas of life and wonder. Both Faith and Prayer soar, they bring us to the living waters of baptism, our life in Christ.

## Take Time to Ponder

This final journey's reflection leaves us with the lifelong task of ongoing adult faith formation and our call to prayer and study. I am always amazed at how many people in their forties and up regret not having a better understanding of faith and out of a sense of embarrassment try to mask this. On the other hand, the under forties can often either think they know it all and resort to dogmatism or tell themselves it is unimportant and escape into atheism or agnosticism. The eunuch represents our incomplete faith, our immature faith that longs to be complete, but cannot. Ask yourself if your faith has been stunted, arrested at the level you were as a kindergartner, or a grade-schooler or high-schooler. Has your faith been neutered, like the eunuch, not really fully mature and not really adult? Do you settle for a make-believe faith or do you journey on a desert road ready to engage a deeper level of meaning, a deeper purpose in life? Reading

59

books on the spiritual life can help, but be sure you read things of substance. I frequently recommend to young and old alike that at some point in life one must read *The Confessions* of St. Augustine (c. 354 – 430). So many people have been profoundly impacted by reading the early Church writers who over twenty centuries ago grappled to understand the Christian life. Happily, these are all available on line at sites like www.newadvent.org (as well as the *Summa* of St. Thomas Aquinas).

Philip represents the adult call to faith that wisely encounters the mystery of God and wants to understand. Remarkably even the desert road has water, enough to impart divine life upon the eunuch as well as upon us. I am afraid that for many people there is a tendency to shy away from the world of thoughts and ideas, to avoid this desert road. Some have even criticized Americans for being anti-intellectual and "dummied down." This is unfortunate because in my years of teaching I can testify to how powerful it is for a person to come to those aha moments. Some days you can even see a person change right before your eyes. Very often in life it is the desert road that holds the deepest insight into who we are and who we strive to become.

St. Thomas Aquinas had a remarkable sense about study as play, the intellectual joy that comes when things connect. Even so, he also had a profound sense of what it takes to be a learner. I have on an old prayer card from years ago that has a prayer for students attributed to St. Thomas. I think it is the perfect prayer for our journey to Gaza, this desert road.

> Come, Holy Spirit, Divine Creator, true source of light and fountain of wisdom! Pour forth your brilliance upon my dense intellect, dissipate the darkness which covers me, that of sin and of ignorance.

Grant me a penetrating mind to understand, a retentive memory, method and ease in learning, the lucidity to comprehend, and abundant grace in expressing myself. Guide the beginning of my work, direct its progress, and bring it to successful completion.

This I ask through Jesus Christ, true God and true man, living and reigning with You and the Father, forever and ever. Amen.

# Conclusion

Being on the way (*in via*) captures our faith journey in this life and prepares us for our ultimate destiny. Though no one really knows what lies beyond a person's final hour, faith assures us of two things: (1) that we have been created for a purpose, and (2) we are ordered to the ultimate good. This is why journey stories are so powerful. Being "on the way" is a moral adventure and each hour, each step of the journey discloses both who we are and where we are headed.

Much can be found in the gospel journeys we just examined. The Gospel itself is a journey story of promise, birth, fear, healing, destiny, discovery, conversion and understanding. These journey stories enable us to find in the journey story of our own life, the footprints of ultimate meaning. The spiritual life opens us to the something more in life. It offers us the fragrance of God's abiding presence that assures us of a nearness, a connection with the divine.

Meister Eckhart wrote, "God is in the homeland and we, we are in the far country." Every medieval pilgrim knew that their journey was twofold: outward to the Holy Land or sacred shrine, and inward, back to the homeland. It is in the far country, the pilgrim's journey, where the soul encounters its purpose. For some people the pilgrimage was in restitution for their sins, for others it was the fulfilling of a vow, and others it was the adventure. Their journey stories remind us all of the profound depth of the human soul and its capacity to encounter the mystery of God.

Now the journey is yours. Allow your steps to disclose to you the way that God is with you "on the way" for in this life we truly walk by faith.

WE WALK BY FAITH

Made in the USA
Columbia, SC
24 January 2020